prosperity consciousness for women

A 12-STEP GUIDE TO CREATE FINANCIAL FLOW

BY SUSAN LOWENTHAL AXELROD

**Prosperity Consciousness for Women:
A 12-Step Guide to Create Financial Flow**

ISBN: 979-8-218-85316-7

First Edition - November 2025

Published by JGU Press. Printed in the USA.

Design & Layout by Carasmatic Design - www.CarasmaticDesign.com

CONTENTS

Preface 6

Introduction: Prosperity Can Be Yours 12

Step One: The Flow of Money 18
Money flows through my financial accounts.

Step Two: Conscious Abundance 24
I am open to receiving, there is enough.

Step Three: On Financial Flow 30
Financial abundance comes easily to me. I receive it with love, confidence, and gratitude.

Step Four: Surprise Yourself 36
I enjoy learning about finances and investments. I study one thing about money every day.

Step Five: Being Specific 42
My accounts are filled with the money I want.

Step Six: The Power of Thoughtful, Strategic, & Disciplined Action 48
I am thoughtful, strategic, and disciplined about activities that generate money flowing into my established accounts.

Step Seven: Be Accountable 54
I model financial responsibility for my children (for others).

Step Eight: Systems Yield Financial Progress 60
I set up a simple and effective system to support my prosperous growth and a resulting yield.

Step Nine: Practice, Practice, Practice 66
I learn about money every day.

Step Ten: Find Focus 72
Focus on what you want.

Step Eleven: Patience Pays Off 78
I take a long view for a prosperous return.

Step Twelve: Trust in Yourself 84
I believe I can.

BONUS Affirmation/Tool: Structure Leads to Success 90
The calendar keeps me on a prosperous track

Conclusion: Are you ready for financial flow? 98

Appendices 100

PREFACE

How much do you pay attention to the work you have put out into the world? When you are an inspired creator, material flows. Often, you put it out and quickly forget about it, moving on to the next (and next) thing. Recently, I was reviewing my own archived material and came across a 24-week Prosperity Consciousness Program I created years ago for a women's leadership group, encouraging them to think more specifically about money and to think more positively about their personal prosperity. It was developed from work I had done in this area for more than 15 years. I read through the material and realized how resonant it was today.

While some women end up with money (through divorce, widowhood, inheritance, or career/earnings), and others end up living in poverty (the National Women's Law Center: "More than one in 10 women lived in poverty in 2024."), all women can use a boost in mindset about money, abundance, and prosperity. Research shows that women are reluctant to work with external financial managers, and that often, women's money is sitting in low or no-interest savings or checking accounts. Also, women self-report lower confidence in their own financial decision-making and investment acumen.

Why is this important? Because when women have money, they support family, community, and humanity. And, wow, does humanity need support today.

So, I came upon my original material, read through it, and reintegrated it. I wanted to rework it into something relevant and useful. But, how? I edited it down for ideas that would stand the test of time, and I used AI for concept development and to help me keep it brief. I have learned about the benefit of small books – easy to read, retain, and especially to apply the information. That's what my readers have told me: "I keep the book by my bed and read a chapter a night for inspiration." "I love the short chapters and writing pages so I can capture what I think about after I read." "I use your chapters as journaling prompts."

As I read the original material – 24 Affirmations with content and context to apply them – I laughed a bit at myself for the prolific nature of my output. Wow, it's good to be in an intuitive, purpose-filled space and share with other smart women! When you allow yourself to be guided by your soul's intuition, outcomes are quick and easy. I whittled the 24 Affirmations down to 12 and created the material in this book for you to contemplate. My Intention is for you to get on a path to a prosperous life. Why? Is money everything? Well, no, money isn't everything, but let's be honest, it's important.

So, is Prosperity Consciousness only about money? No, it's about an abundant mindset and a belief system that generates prosperous manifestation. I have used Affirmations as a tool successfully to transform my mindset and experience for nearly 50 years. To affirm is to state as a fact; to assert strongly and publicly. Before the idea was mainstreamed in the 1800s and early 1900s as 'conscious autosuggestion,' Affirmations were an ancient tradition. One example of this is prayer, another example is meditation, where you affirm a sacred syllable. I was introduced to Affirmations through Napoleon Hill, Bob Proctor, Louise Hay, and Wayne Dyer. I learned about the power of the mind, I practiced diligently, and I was astounded by the results.

APPLY

As a Coach, I work with clients in mindset transformation. For successful integration, I always 'Apply'. Tune in as you go through your day. What are the thoughts you're thinking about money? Are they positive and supportive, or based on worry, fear, and resistance? Here's an Affirmation for you to start your practice now:

Mindset Matters | *My personal economy rises and falls with my abundance mindset. I keep my personal abundance mindset high.*

This affirmation is radically important for women, especially when it comes to wealth, prosperity, and self-worth. It reclaims power from external economies, like recessions, inflation, layoffs, and pay gaps, which can feel overwhelming and uncontrollable, especially for women, as we already navigate economic inequality. This affirmation reminds us that while the outer world affects us, our inner financial ecosystem—mindsets, beliefs, and expectations—drives our personal economy. It's a shift from helplessness to agency. Your mindset is the economy over which you have the most control.

Mindset drives financial decisions. An abundance mindset doesn't mean wishful thinking or ignoring reality; it means believing there is enough, and that you are enough, to create wealth. Women with an abundance mindset are more likely to ask for raises, invest with confidence, start businesses, learn about wealth-building, and say 'Yes!' to opportunities. A scarcity mindset shrinks decisions. An abundance mindset expands them.

This affirmation ties your personal economy directly to your mental and emotional state—which means it must be tended to daily. It's not just about money. It's about self-belief, gratitude, openness to receive, and trusting yourself to handle and grow money. *"I keep my abundance mindset high"* becomes a ritual. A reset. A choice you make again and again.

Acknowledging emotional and cultural baggage that we often carry is important. Thoughts such as: "There's never enough." "I shouldn't want too much." "Money is for men to handle." "I'm not good with numbers." This affirmation challenges those old beliefs, helping you to create your own financial atmosphere.

Abundance starts with how you think, feel, and

receive. Don't wait for wealth to feel abundant; train your mindset to be fertile ground for it. "My personal economy rises and falls with my abundance mindset" isn't a metaphor—it's the truth. People who think abundantly, act abundantly, and that's what grows wealth.

Let this affirmation be a compass showing you the way and reminding you that while the world may shift, mindset remains your anchor. It's not naive, it's strategic. When you keep your abundance mindset high, you cultivate resilience, power, and prosperity from the inside out. As you build this resilience, your spiritual, mental, emotional, and financial accounts will grow.

reflection

What beliefs have I inherited about money being difficult, scarce, or "not for me?" How would my decisions change if I truly believed that money flows through my accounts with ease and purpose?

INTRODUCTION

Prosperity Can Be Yours

Dear Reader,

What does prosperity mean to you? Here's the dictionary definition:

Prosperity: the state of being prosperous
Prosperous: successful in material terms; flourishing financially

And the word consciousness? While it is a big concept, the simple definition is:

Consciousness: the quality or state of being aware, especially of something within oneself

Then, the term Prosperity Consciousness would be defined as: *The state of being aware of success in material terms, of flourishing financially*

Whether you purchased this book or received it as a gift and are reading it, the title must have resonated with you. The definitions above ensure our mutual understanding of this work.

So, *are* you aware of being successful materially or of flourishing financially? And these clarifying questions (be honest with yourself):

- As you think about this idea, do you shy away from it? (Why?)
- Do you find that you have a belief that 'I shouldn't talk about money,' 'I shouldn't want money,' or that 'Money is the root of all evil'?

I started studying this topic in the late 1990s. My sister shared an audio series she had purchased called "Prosperity Consciousness, How to tap your unlimited wealth." It was a cassette tape set published by Nightingale-Conant in 1994, from a live course presented by Fredric Lehrman in 1993. I began studying the topic then, and have never stopped.

In 2019, I wrote to Fredric Lehrman to ask him to explain the use of the terms prosperity consciousness and abundance mindset. I asked him if they were different. Here is how he answered:

> *"Both 'Prosperity Consciousness' and 'Abundance Mindset' are just words pointing to the same area of awareness. I didn't make up either one of them, but the first use of Prosperity Consciousness was when Nightingale-Conant wanted to give my course that title based on a series of questions sent out to their in-house focus groups back in 1993. I had been teaching my workshop since 1975 under the title, "Getting Money Right: the psychology of wealth." It's more grounded*

and specific, but any one of the three choices is accurate in its own way."

I interpreted his response as this: 'it's all in there.' And I've been teaching it that way since.

HOW TO USE THIS BOOK

This book is a 12-Step Guide to your prosperous mindset. I chose 12 steps because of the calendar (not because of the Addiction Recovery program). I learned a long time ago to make the calendar my friend, and that its universal nature transcends any divides. My original concept was to suggest that you spend one month learning, practicing, and integrating each Affirmation for a 'year-long program.' As I worked with the Affirmations myself and started developing this manuscript, I realized that people would go at their own pace – perhaps reviewing one Affirmation daily or weekly instead of monthly. However you choose, the path is yours to take.

Key, however, is that you read, review, practice, and integrate the material. Each Affirmation stands on its own. It is not necessary to learn them in the order presented in the book, but I worked to create a progression leading to the twelfth Affirmation that will set you on a new, prosperous path. Here's a map for you:

1. Make your plan. Skim through the whole book first.

See what resonates with you. Think about why you are reading the book, and what you would like to see as a result of getting through this 12-Step Program. Changing your ideas and understanding of the topic matter is possible; it takes work and commitment for transformation to occur.

2. Map it out. After you've skimmed through the book, consider and decide how you would like to map your learning and integration of the material. What could you do in 12 days? What would happen with weekly review over 12 weeks? Or, do you want to commit to working with each Affirmation over a month and progressing forward through an entire year, knowing that you will have a transformed mindset at the end? There's no correct answer; as long as you consider your map and take action now.

3. Find a partner. This is a key step that will support your path and progress. Without a working partner on the same journey with the same intention, you may get stalled. Find someone who gets it and is excited to partner with you. Your mutual enthusiasm will make a difference in your outcomes; be accountable to your future, financially solvent selves! A note here from personal experience. Don't attempt to shove your spouse or partner into this role. Don't want it for them while they are in resistance. I get it (I do). But all the wishing in the world doesn't change another person. Instead, start your own abundance mindset now and go with someone who is aligned with growing in this way. And, while you're at it, don't judge your spouse or partner.

4. Fail Forward. When you fail in your plan, shake it off and move forward. Either start again, or continue from where you left off. The effort will be rewarded. Don't allow the small issue of failure to derail you! If you fail, fail forward. Get back to it, stick with it, keep at it. This is an abundance mindset itself!

5. Handwrite notes in the book or in your journal. "Research shows that handwriting and typing engage different cognitive and neural mechanisms, with implications from both evolutionary and neuroscientific perspectives. From a neuroscientific perspective, studies have shown that handwriting engages the sensorimotor cortex, visual areas, and language centres (e.g., Broca's area) more extensively than typing."[1] Personally, I can attest to the power of handwriting. I have nearly 30 handwritten journals, most of them containing written visualizations, Affirmations, intentions, and deep desires. Don't let handwriting become a lost art for you; support your brain and your outcomes by writing out notes while also supporting integration of the material.

BEFORE YOU GET STARTED

Before you get into the book, here is an important journaling exercise for you. Be sure to do it, don't skip this preliminary step. Ask yourself these questions:

---

1. https://pmc.ncbi.nlm.nih.gov/articles/PMC11943480/

- Do I believe it's ok to be wealthy?
- Do I believe that I deserve to be wealthy?
- Do I believe that being wealthy is good or bad?

These questions might seem strange or even ridiculous to you, but I answered them myself when I got started with prosperity consciousness decades ago. As the years have passed, with life's twists and turns inevitably involving money and finances, I have revisited these questions repeatedly. All energy-based, consciousness-raising activity is a practice. Yoga, breathing, Qigong, meditation, prayer, fitness, and so on. Life can be fraught, and no matter how grounded we are, we are likely to veer off the path along the way. No worries, pick yourself up, and keep practicing.

At the outset of my study, I learned that Fredric Lehrman's basic notion is about handling your money in a conscious way, not letting anxiety interfere with the way you're relating to money in your life. Remember, prosperity consciousness is the state of being aware of success in material terms, or of flourishing financially.

Wishing you the best always,
Susan

DISCLAIMER-This book is not intended to give financial advice. It is intended to help you face and challenge your thoughts about money, break through any resistance you feel to topics such as money, wealth, finances, or investments, and open your mindset to become confident and comfortable becoming wealthy.

THE FLOW OF MONEY

Money flows through my financial accounts.

Does this Affirmation resonate with you? Or, can you feel the resistance even as you read it? Both responses are OK. If the Affirmation resonates, that means you are already in good alignment with the flow of money, but you still bought this book to improve your prosperity consciousness, that will happen. If the Affirmation does not resonate with you, it's OK. You bought this book to get onto that path, this will happen.

The language of "flow" is especially powerful when it comes to money. It evokes ease, abundance, and natural movement – a stark contrast to the struggle, guilt, or anxiety many women have been conditioned to feel around finances. For women who were taught to downplay their financial desires or prioritize others' needs over their own, the idea that *money flows through my accounts* can feel radical – and healing.

Attributing flow to money shifts money from something to control, hoard, or fear into something alive: a renewable resource that moves with grace. It allows women to begin seeing money not as a source of tension or shame, but as an ally – something that can be earned, saved, invested, used without guilt, and enjoyed. The use of the word 'through' in the Affirmation is intentional. Through depicts the idea of circulating, coming in, and going out. For flow to happen, there needs to be kinetic energy (in motion), not static energy (stored, stopped). Money will flow in and grow, and it will be spent in support of the economy. Women clients tell me that they want more money to spend on family, experiences, education, and well-being. All of these things improve our world.

Affirmations are most powerful when paired with an intentional mindset and specific actions, such as financial education, planning, and aligned choices. Flow results when mindset and movement work together; transformation becomes not only possible, but inevitable. Doing other activities in your life to increase flow will support your desired results. Mindful movement, fit-life activity, anything creative (art, singing, dancing, writing, praying), and especially getting quiet within, will help you realize the blockages to the flow of your energy. Any, or better, all of these activities will support your flow.

Flow results when mindset and movement work together.

For money to flow into and through your financial accounts, you need to understand what flow is, what it feels like, and how it works out for you. Again, an intentional mindset paired with specific actions leads to desired outcomes. This Affirmation is about the flow of money, not about how much you have. Often, it's the 'how much' question that stops the flow. For now, just let it flow.

reflection

What beliefs have I inherited about money being difficult, scarce, or "not for me?" How would my decisions change if I truly believed that money flows through my accounts with ease and purpose?

22 • Money flows freely to me.

CONSCIOUS ABUNDANCE

I am open to receiving, there is enough.

Are you…open to receiving, though? Do you believe that there is enough to go around for everyone? Consider these questions. Many women give endlessly but resist receiving. If your heart isn't open to receive, how can your wallet be? Your finances reflect your energy. Negative beliefs — like feeling guilty about money, thinking it's greedy to want more, or believing you shouldn't be paid for your gifts or abilities — often stem from childhood conditioning. Ask yourself: Do I deserve to be supported?

Imagine how much more impact you could make if you were coming from a place of abundance, self-support, from believing in your Self. This one shift can change everything. When you truly affirm receiving, you'll feel your heart, mind, and love expand in ways you never expected.

If you let these words take root, they can transform your entire relationship with prosperity. Let this be more than a mantra — make it a conversation. Sit with yourself. Gently challenge the scarcity stories you've inherited or absorbed. Scarcity conditioning runs deep. It whispers that there's not enough money, time, love, or space — that you're behind, lacking, or undeserving of receiving. But these beliefs aren't truths; they're patterns of thought. And patterns can be reprogrammed.

Women are often socialized at a young age to be the primary nurturers and givers in families and relationships, and become the same in workplaces. Many become so focused on giving that they struggle to receive help, compliments, gifts, or opportunities when offered. Do you have an "I can do it myself" mentality? This might be a protective mechanism, but this Affirmation can block you from receiving support, collaboration, or resources that could help you thrive.

If you rush through Affirmations without connecting to their emotional truth, they become hollow rituals. But if you do the spiritual and emotional work to let them resonate deeply, the words become a quiet revolution in your mind, stemming panic, softening fear, and opening the door to peace.

There is enough. Enough money. Enough love. Enough food. Enough time. Enough opportunity. Enough space. Enough for me. I am worthy of receiving.

Gently challenge the scarcity stories you've inherited.

When you don't believe this, you're not just lacking resources – you're living in resistance to life itself. Scarcity consciousness locks you in fear, and that fear leads to emotional turmoil, anxiety, exhaustion, hopelessness – and in some cases, even physical illness.

This Affirmation gently reminds you: you are not alone, you are not empty, and you are worthy. This one belief rewires the brain toward abundance, and that shift begins to reflect outward – in your choices, relationships, finances, and future. As you open in this way, you will also open to receiving money that will flow through your accounts.

reflection

In what area of your life do you most often feel there isn't enough or that it is hard to receive — money, time, energy, love, recognition? Consider this, then reflect, changing the idea from this: there isn't enough, to this: What would it feel like if there is enough? How would it feel to receive it easily?

28 • Money flows freely to me.

ON FINANCIAL FLOW

Financial abundance comes easily to me.
I receive it with love, confidence, and gratitude.

Do you have systems to manage your money? Where will it go if you don't have a place for it to land 'easily'? Set up your own personal, not joint, savings sub-account now and title it My Financial Account. Put in $1,000, $100, or $10. Whatever is realistic or possible. If you do this today and put in $20 every week, you'll have $1000 or more from this financial practice. A year from now, what could you do with a 'found' $1,000? This is abundance! It would be your own money. Spend it on the kids, or on yourself, or become a philanthropist! Give away $1,000 to a mission that speaks to your soul! Likely, you already easily spend an average of $20 a week on coffee out, nails, or an app on your phone. What if you saved more now to spend on your mindset, education, well-being, or your business instead?

The intentional practice of establishing a system for managing your money cultivates a healthy, positive relationship with money, rather than one based on fear, scarcity, or shame. This emotional shift often precedes practical financial improvements and freedom around money. This is financial abundance coming easily to you.

Many women are socialized to be givers rather than receivers, often feeling uncomfortable or guilty when good things come to them. The affirmation "I receive it with love" helps normalize and celebrate receiving abundance rather than deflecting or minimizing it. Adding confidence helps counteract the imposter syndrome many women experience when money comes to them — the feeling that they don't belong in spaces of financial abundance.

This is an Affirmation that changed my life. But only when I started seeing abundance in ways that were different from what I was taught growing up. It took learning a new thought, deep reflection, time, and practice to break the old thought pattern of having to work hard in order to get rewarded. I worked consciously at this one, learning to see resources — not just money — as a form of abundance. For example, if I needed or wanted something, and if someone gave it to me, I no longer saw it as random, but rather as abundance coming to me; game-changer.

It is an old message that women who pursue or

Confidently acknowledge and embrace your financial wins.

accumulate wealth are somehow selfish or unfeminine. "With love" and "gratitude" reframes financial abundance as something positive and aligned with caring values, not something that makes you greedy or cold. Were you taught to be modest about success and downplay achievements? This Affirmation encourages you to confidently acknowledge and embrace your financial wins.

The combination of love, confidence, and gratitude creates a warm, secure emotional container for financial abundance. This helps reduce the anxiety or fear that can unconsciously block financial opportunities. Move beyond seeing your accounts grow from relying solely on traditional employment, and realize the boon of other resources. Eventually, you will see abundance, opportunity, and resources everywhere.

reflection

What would it feel like to be in an abundance mindset, to receive easily, and to know you will make good decisions about it from a place of informed personal confidence?

34 • Money flows freely to me.

SURPRISE YOURSELF

I enjoy learning about finances and investments. I study one thing about money every day.

Wealthy people pay attention to the stock market and learn the basics of finance and investing. Generating income does not create prosperity, investment does. If you don't commit to learning this topic area, you will never get on top of your financial picture. Don't wait until you have money to invest. Start learning about it now. Investopedia might be a place to start or the Financial Awareness Foundation (both have quality, free information).* And teach your children, too. Create the vessel of learning and make it enjoyable for them.

Why study about money every day? Because what you focus on, you achieve. Every Time. This can be tested with anything. Look at the things you've accomplished recently — how did you complete them? Was it something you deeply wanted? Had to do?

Needed badly? Whatever the reason, it's likely you thought about it every day. That's what the second part of this affirmation is about – setting up a system where you learn something about money every day keeps it present, current in your mind, and relevant to your life.

Learning about finances and investments reverses generational financial conditioning. Historically, many women were socialized to avoid or defer financial decision-making to others – partners, fathers, or professionals. This affirmation flips that narrative, putting women in the driver's seat of their financial education. By claiming "I enjoy learning," it reframes finance from something stressful or intimidating into something empowering and even enjoyable.

This statement is a wake-up call, 'Generating income does not create prosperity; investment does.' Many women focus on saving or earning a stable income, but not enough on investing for long-term wealth. The idea is not just to work hard, but rather to make money work for you through smart investing. Single, married, divorced, widowed, old, or young...every woman needs financial literacy to ensure her security and to feel empowered about money. This goes beyond basic budgeting and awareness about debt. Studying the basics of compound interest and about how stocks, bonds, annuities, and mutual funds work is not optional; it's a cornerstone of financial autonomy.

Learn the basics of finance and investing.

When a woman learns and models financial knowledge, she changes the trajectory not just for herself, but also for her children. They will grow up seeing her be bold and will see investing as normal, not mysterious or male-dominated. Affirming that learning about finances can be "enjoyed" deconstructs the belief that money is stressful or confusing. Invite a more peaceful, empowered relationship with money, and make the journey less intimidating and more fulfilling.

*I am not affiliated with Investopedia or the Financial Awareness Foundation

reflection

This Affirmation is not just about learning finance—it's about owning power, reclaiming personal space, and building legacy. For women, it turns financial literacy into an act of liberation and leadership. Can you feel it?!

40 • Money flows freely to me.

step 5

BEING SPECIFIC

My financial accounts are filled with the money I want.

You say you want more money – but have you defined what it's for? Have you taken time to write it out and get real clarity? Most people have not. They just want relief – from stress, debt, or the fear of current or future bills. And if you already have more than enough, have you created a Strategic Philanthropy Plan to ensure your wealth creates meaningful impact?

This affirmation gives you permission to have specific financial desires and goals rather than just hoping to "get by" or meet basic needs, a concept sometimes governed by parents or even grandparents from childhood. Many women have been taught that wanting money is shallow or selfish. Having financial ambitions helps women move beyond the "money doesn't matter" conditioning that can keep them financially stuck. Being clear, intentional, and specific is key! We cannot simply wish for it, be quiet about it, or be too vague about our financial targets. What is it that you want?

I admit, this one was hard for me. What did I want? I did quite a bit of work on this and found myself struggling with the type of thinking mentioned above, that the material things I 'wanted' were shallow or selfish. But why? Why do men get 'toys' for themselves and women get toys for our kids or dogs? Over time spent working on this, I played around with questions like: What would I do right now if I had (insert amount here) in my own financial account? Inevitably, at first, I found myself considering house projects, things I wanted for my children's rooms, even college savings accounts. Later, as I grew my own business, it was easy to get more clear. I wanted money to spend on things I needed for business – equipment, conferences, resources – without having to get permission from anyone else. This is when the journaling exercises produced results. I began to 'see' clearly what I wanted and why I wanted my accounts to fill.

Most women are raised to downplay financial success or act like money doesn't matter to them. Instead of just affirming having money, this Affirmation truly pushes you towards abundance and having what you actually desire, not just what you need to survive. This is truly important because traditionally, when

Being clear, intentional, and specific is key!

women have money, they spend it on their families, their communities, and on charity; always in support of others. More recently, we are seeing women spending money on healthy living, education, and self-development while still tending to family, and community, showing the next generation an important sense of self while also supporting others.

NOTE: It is true that later in life, when you have spent the money on your children, pets, family lives, communities, and on work Sunshine Funds, you realize the importance of things money can not buy. But, if you do not have resources, you suffer – always – with worry about paying the necessary bills to support your life. It is a luxury and a privilege late in life, to be able to say, "I don't need much, now."

reflection

Have I clearly defined how much money I want—and what I want it for? Or am I simply wishing for more?

46 • Money flows freely to me.

step 6

THE POWER OF THOUGHTFUL, STRATEGIC, AND DISCIPLINED ACTION

I am thoughtful, strategic, and disciplined about activities that generate money flowing into my established accounts.

This Affirmation addresses several underlying barriers that often limit financial success. Too often, women's financial achievements are attributed to luck or external circumstances rather than recognized as the result of skill, planning, and strategy. This new thought helps reclaim ownership over financial outcomes by emphasizing deliberate action rather than chance. It also challenges the common belief that money is too complicated to manage. Many women have been conditioned to think financial planning is beyond their abilities. Surprisingly, I find this still to be true enough for women in younger generations, often deferring to fathers, then husbands, on financial decisions. Early in my Confidence Coaching practice, I was shocked to speak with several women who were primary income earners, yet who deferred to their male spouses or partners to make financial decisions with the money they were earning.

Countering that narrative, this Affirmation reinforces the idea that women are capable, strategic thinkers who can confidently navigate financial decisions.

For those with irregular income – such as entrepreneurs or women in creative or helping fields – this idea encourages a shift from sporadic earnings to more consistent, structured income. The phrase "*flowing into my established accounts*" reinforces the vision of regular income streams, a solid financial foundation, and systems in place, rather than relying on occasional windfalls or haphazard deposits.

Also, it helps cultivate a sense of business acumen. Describing oneself as thoughtful, strategic, and disciplined affirms a professional identity rooted in intentionality and long-term planning. This is particularly important in a culture where women are often expected to make success appear effortless. The affirmation pushes back against that pressure by acknowledging that real financial success requires consistent effort, clear goals, and a practical approach. This applies to household finances, equally needing thoughtful, strategic, and disciplined activities and systems.

You are fully equipped to manage and grow wealth with purpose.

It also promotes long-term thinking by highlighting the importance of financial infrastructure. References to "established accounts" signal not just present income, but preparation for future growth and wealth-building. By integrating both mindset and behavior, you go beyond surface-level positivity. It encourages you to reflect on how your actions align with your intentions, and to make empowered, income-generating choices with clarity and confidence.

Ultimately, this affirmation helps you form a strong, professional identity as a financially disciplined and strategic individual, both at home and at work. As that identity solidifies, so does the belief – and reality – that you are fully equipped to manage and grow wealth with purpose. You are not too young or too old to learn this new mindset and behavior. Any Belief System can be countered at any time if you have laid the groundwork. Review the prior 5 Affirmations now if necessary to get into a positive mindset for this pivotal shift in your Belief System.

reflection

In what specific area of your financial life have you been attributing your results to luck or external circumstances rather than recognizing your own strategic choices—and what would change if you fully owned that capability?

52 • Money flows freely to me.

BE ACCOUNTABLE

I model financial responsibility for my children (for others).

Have you ever contemplated your money story? Do you have any idea where your ideas about money and wealth come from? Unless you have done any work in this area, all of your ideas about anything connected to money come from your upbringing. Whether you were raised by parents, grandparents, or in a system, the way you act with money was role modeled by someone else. Do you realize this? And sometimes, if our own thoughts and practices are not well-honed, we can be influenced by someone else, even beyond our childhood.

I had a 50-year old woman client who, through our work together, realized that she was still making decisions and choices based on a relationship she was in at age 20, with someone who was 10 years older and therefore influential. This was sobering. A woman in her full maturity making decisions based on who she was when she was 20 years old, influenced by an insecure man who was only 30 years old and had not been in her life for decades. Further, she realized that her own 20-year old daughter was now making her decisions based on her single mother's role modeling.

Does this sound unbelievable to you? Think again. Tune in to your own money story. Whose modeling are you following? Then ask yourself, 'What *am* I modeling regarding money, and financial responsibility?'

Were you taught financial literacy—empowered with the knowledge to create the life you desire without financial strain or regret? Agency over money isn't exclusive to the wealthy. Anyone can learn to be intentional about how mindset combined with action (like setting up systems and saving early) can overcome systemic obstacles over time. You have the power to break free from the belief that women must wait for a partner, an inheritance, or ideal circumstances to take control. You can create new rules for yourself and begin right where you are.

It takes fortitude to move beyond the Belief Systems that stem from the imprint of upbringing that can lead to 'stuckness' in this arena. When a woman takes ownership of her financial future, she changes her own life and teaches by example, shaping the expectations,

You can create new rules for yourself.

confidence, and financial habits of her children – especially daughters. As in the real example given above, mindset models generational impact. With work to uncover old beliefs, and commitment to creating a new paradigm of prosperity, mindset can be changed, new thoughts and practices can be created. This personal growth can lead to generational wealth in money and in mindset.

reflection

What comes up for you when you think of the term 'generational wealth'? Do you immediately say, "That's not me"? If so, that is what you are modeling for your children. What if you asked more neutrally, "Could I create generational wealth for my family going forward if I change the way I think about things and develop new practices and systems?" How does this resonate with you?

58 • Money flows freely to me.

step 8

SYSTEMS YIELD FINANCIAL PROGRESS

I set up simple and effective systems to support my prosperous growth and a resulting yield.

When it comes to financial success, systems matter. But the way women are taught about systems often differs significantly from men. Boys are more likely to be exposed to linear, goal-oriented structures, while girls are typically shown non-linear, relational systems, such as caregiving roles. You might ask, "In this day and age?!" My answer is yes. I see this in my Confidence Coaching work with women of all ages, including many young professionals of our time who are still largely (but not exclusively) responsible for the home. Domestic or household systems, though foundational, are rarely framed as "real systems" or acknowledged for their strategic value. This difference in framing can impact how women approach money and long-term financial planning.

What were you taught about building financial infrastructure to support your financial life? Do you manage money reactively—paying bills as they arrive, dealing with issues only when they become urgent? Do you find yourself waiting for your husband or partner to weigh in on financial issues or concerns, even when they are in your domain? This can stem from the practices of your family, or because he has 'trained' you in the way he was trained, or because you think it's 'fair' to involve him in financial decisions, likely because this is the way you want to be treated.

This topic comes up regularly in my coaching practice. 'She' might have ideas and plans but for some reason waits for 'him' to agree or take action. Why? Likely, this is what she absorbed in her family of origin, her father making the decisions based on his systems and the mother having to wait, or argue to get her way. I lived in this paradigm myself, I know it well. Breaking free from it started my own path to prosperity consciousness 25 years ago. Now, I have worked on this issue with dozens of women clients.

Often, conflict ensues because money mindsets and practices are different for women, but also because women do not want to argue, a common unpleasant outcome most want to avoid. But systems support neutrality ('there's a system for this, let's follow it'). Neutrality supports a proactive shift to self-empowerment. For you to consciously design systems that support sustainable financial progress, puts you in

Consciously design systems that support sustainable financial progress.

charge and helps instill confidence to make decisions on your own, without waiting or feeling you have to get permission. It also helps overcome the fear or resistance that systems must be overly complex. Using the words "simple and effective," reinforces that clarity and ease are not only possible, but essential.

Creating and using systems empowers you to see yourself as a builder of wealth, managing, investing, and multiplying that money over time. The phrase "growth and resulting yield," reinforces the importance of patience, discipline, and structure. Wealth-building doesn't happen overnight – it's cultivated through systems that support financial momentum and compound over time. Ultimately, you can be the architect of your own financial future with simple and effective systems.

reflection

What systems can I put in place now to support my financial progress? And what internal beliefs or external habits might be preventing me from establishing them?

step 9

PRACTICE, PRACTICE, PRACTICE

I learn about money every day.

Any form of mastery comes through consistent practice. People who build and sustain wealth understand this. Historically, many first-generation wealth builders lived by this principle: they read, asked questions, stayed curious, applied through trial and error, saved, and developed financial literacy and success over time. But in many cases, they did not pass on these practices because of the patriarchal myth that 'it's not polite to talk about money.' Therefore, second and third generation inheritors often lacked the same discipline and understanding, leading to the collapse of family businesses and fortunes.

Curiosity and discipline to learn something about money every day is a powerful intention. It emphasizes that financial empowerment is not innate — it is cultivated. Despite how central money is to your daily life, how much do you know about how it works? How much do you really understand about budgeting, saving, real estate investing, the stock market, compound growth, interest rates, tax implications, variable vs fixed returns, i.e., creating a foundation for your own financial security?

As with most things today, money systems are now blind. Things happen in the background in our devices as if by magic. We are not required to put in any effort for anything to happen. Most of us program in automation for income and expenses, leave it and forget it, halting active learning which builds knowledge and confidence.

Historically, women have been excluded from financial conversations. Many women did not grow up hearing about investments, business strategies, or wealth-building in clubs, on the golf course, or at the office. Surprisingly, this still holds true today. Women often abdicate on this topic to men in their lives. This Affirmation helps close that gap by creating a daily commitment to financial growth. It also challenges the deeply ingrained myth that women are "not numbers people." By learning a little every day, women can actively dismantle that false belief reframing money as something to explore with curiosity rather than avoid out of fear or confusion.

When approached in manageable daily steps, financial literacy becomes accessible and empowering, and reinforces the idea that expertise is built gradually. No one becomes a financial expert overnight. With

If you practice daily financial learning, you will inspire those around you.

consistency, you can begin to claim your space, traditionally dominated by men, in financial conversations and decisions. As you become more informed, you reduce financial dependence on others and gain the ability to advocate for yourself, negotiate wisely, and make strategic decisions.

If you practice daily financial learning, you will inspire those around you. You model what it looks like to be financially curious, capable, and confident. And because the financial world is constantly changing, with new investment tools, shifting economic policies, and evolving opportunities, ongoing learning ensures that you remain agile and informed. Make it a habit. Read financial news. Listen to podcasts. Discuss money openly. Turn it into a game with your children and normalize the idea that money is not only good — it's a powerful tool that supports our lives and expands our ability to help others.

reflection

What practices am I ready to create for a prosperous, empowered mindset? How can I transform financial education into a daily lifestyle that builds long-term confidence and capability? Where is a good place to start my new practice of learning daily?

70 • Money flows freely to me.

FIND FOCUS

Focus on what you want.

One of the simplest, yet most life-changing truths on the journey to prosperity consciousness is this: *What you focus on, you achieve.* It's deceptively simple—and profoundly powerful. You will not progress beyond this step if you do not learn this principle. Most of us spend far too much time focusing on what we lack, what went wrong, what has not happened, or what failed. That kind of thinking keeps us stuck. Instead, train your mind to return — again and again — to what you want regarding money and prosperous living (go back to Step 5 if you need). If something did not go as planned, if the money did not come in as you expected, review it, learn from it, and try again. But never lose sight of your vision. Focusing on what you want pulls you forward; focusing on what you lack keeps you standing still.

What is it that you want? If you want money, focus on

that. If you want to be financially secure, focus on that. If you want to be financially *free*, focus on that. If you want to get smarter or more adept at managing your wealth creation, focus on wealth creation. This Affirmation helps dismantle one of the most persistent cultural, and psychological patterns that limit financial success and fulfillment for women. Women are often conditioned to prioritize the needs and wants of others – whether as caretakers, partners, or professionals – leaving their own desires buried, unclear, or unfocused.

This practice gives you permission to identify and pursue what you truly want. It also helps you break free from the myth that wanting more is selfish. Consider this, do you feel uncomfortable focusing on your own goals? Give thought to why that is. In reality, knowing what you want–and allowing yourself to move toward it – is not only healthy, it is essential for building a meaningful and authentic life.

Additionally, many women are trapped in a loop of focusing on problems or fears. This focus on what's wrong drains energy and blocks growth. Shifting attention toward desired outcomes strengthens clarity, motivation, and confidence. It also addresses a common cause of indecision: not knowing what you truly want leads to inaction, default choices, or settling for less than you deserve. When you consistently focus on what you want – specific financial goals, meaningful work, time freedom, a space of your own, abundance – you activate your personal agency. You begin to move with purpose.

What you focus on, you achieve.

You begin to build a life aligned with your values, not just the expectations of others.

This foundational work empowers women to reclaim their right to dream, desire, and design lives that truly reflect who they are, supported by the necessary financial resources.

reflection

What do I truly want—not what I've been told to want, or what feels safe, or what others expect, but what I deeply and honestly desire? And how can I start focusing more clearly and consistently on that vision each day?

76 • Money flows freely to me.

PATIENCE PAYS OFF

I take a long view for a prosperous return.

What would it feel like to step out of urgency? Then, if you do step out of urgency, what are you stepping into? Grounded, sustainable growth. True wealth—whether financial, emotional, or spiritual—is rarely built overnight. While transformation can happen in an instant, *staying* in a prosperous position requires time, consistency, and intentional care. This long view relieves the pressure to have everything figured out immediately. It allows for grace in the journey.

Many women are raised to prioritize short-term survival—making ends meet, reacting to needs, caring for others—without being taught how to build long-term financial security. Cultural expectations often encourage women to put others' futures before their own, delaying personal financial planning or wealth creation. I have had several women clients who supported husbands through various academic or professional programs, only to end up divorced without their own higher-level credentials, promotions earned at work, or financial savings. Other women have spent down an inheritance to support the family, again suffering total loss upon the divorce. Still other women have husbands who spend recklessly on toys, hobbies, or addiction, putting the family in jeopardy before leaving them behind in the financial dust when they implode in some way. These stories shock me deeply each time, but have been shared consistently with me over many years. They were part of the impetus for me to write this book.

Women deserve prosperity, and the grace of understanding that achieving it takes time. When women begin to earn, save, and manage their money with a long-term vision, they shift from reactive patterns into powerful, proactive financial leadership. One of my coaching lessons – one that changed my own life – is this reflection: 'Time is passing anyway.' My life changed when I started *doing the things* that I used to dream about while *not doing them* (did you get that?). I got on the path, stayed on the path, veered off the path, and actively, with intention, sought a way forward.

The long view also helps normalize fluctuations. Small dips in income, focus, or financial progress do not mean failure, they are part of the curve. What matters most is the upward trajectory over time. When you trust that the seeds you are planting now – whether investments, business efforts, or new money habits – will yield returns

Grace in the journey.

in the future, you are less likely to panic and more likely to stay committed to your path.

Taking the long view empowers women to move out of scarcity, into strategy and onto action. It builds resilience, patience, and belief in the compounding value of their actions. Wealth is not just about quick wins; it's about a life of sustained abundance mindset, built with clarity, vision, and faith in the process.

reflection

How can I begin to trust the long view of my financial journey (remember Step 4)—and what can I do today that my future self will thank me for?

82 • Money flows freely to me.

TRUST IN YOURSELF

I believe I can.

Do you? Believe you can change the way you think about money? Do you believe there is enough and that you can have money flowing freely through your accounts? Do you believe you can have the things money will buy that you have yearned for? Do you believe you can set up smart systems, focus, be patient, learn about financial vehicles, and benefit from prosperous returns?

In my own transformation journey, I learned the power of the Belief System, and that knowing your own mindset matters (reread the Preface if needed). This last step is the final breakthrough, and a final test for yourself. What do you believe about yourself?

Check in with what comes to your mind about money matters and your financial picture. Do you have a thought about 'not being good with money'? If so, do you know where this came from? As you drill down here, keep asking yourself intentionally, 'Do I believe I can?' When you challenge yourself in this way, you will activate a new Belief System about finances and prosperity. Belief is the foundation of personal agency, which leads to the impetus to take action. Taking action can transform your financial future.

Many women subconsciously doubt their financial capabilities. This can be due to cultural, societal, or familial conditioning. Thoughts like "Investing is too risky/ confusing for me," or "I'm too emotional when it comes to money" get created as common internal narratives. "I believe I can" begins to break that mental ceiling. It fosters self-trust, replacing internalized doubt and paving the way for positive financial actions such as budgeting, investing, or confidently asking for a raise.

All change begins with belief. Whether it's opening your first brokerage account, tackling debt, or starting a business, this Affirmation is what gives permission to try. Without belief, even the best tools or advice won't lead to change. This mental investment precedes the financial one.

Women often face systemic barriers in wealth-building: the gender pay gap, fewer financial education opportunities, longer lifespans (requiring more savings), and underrepresentation in financial conversations and leadership. This affirmation is a personal stand against those external limitations. It's a declaration of worth, capability, and intention, regardless of what the outside world says.

All change begins with belief.

Money decisions often require courage — to take risks, to be visible, to make mistakes, and to learn. "I believe I can" is a shield against fear. It helps women move through uncertainty with the knowledge that even if the path is unfamiliar, they are capable.

reflection

This affirmation is a quiet revolution. It's how you start to rewrite your financial story—not by waiting for the perfect time or conditions, but by deciding that your potential is real, right now. It's the mindset that turns hope into action—and action into prosperity. How do you want to start your next financial chapter? [Do you believe you can?]

88 • Money flows freely to me.

EASY SUCCESS

The calendar keeps me on a prosperous track.

Learning to use the calendar as my partner helped me immeasurably in life and business. In my old Type A days, time was my enemy. Eventually, giving up the 'busy' bragging rights brought my nervous system into better balance. I learned the magic of these numbers: 365, 52, 12, 6, 4, 1. Days, Weeks, months, bimonthly, quarters, annually. I would ask myself, 'For this task, activity, or responsibility, how do I want to map this based on its importance to me?' Whatever the answer, I mapped it out manually in my trusty paper *Daytimer* for years, and eventually moved to the digital calendar with automated reminders.

Discipline goes with this tool. You can do detailed planning and mapping, but if you don't use the tool, it's a time-waster. Plotting in automated reminders between your calendar and your phone can support productivity if you are in good nervous system balance, in awareness, and in charge of your *Self*.* If you're overwhelmed, not even good tools will support you.

Wait....you can use your own calendar to set specific financial growth goals, have automated motivational reminders, and keep on a prosperous track?

Yes! You can (I've done it). Is it easy? Not so much for women. If you color-code a woman's calendar, assigning colors for each person (family member or employee), and assigning more colors for the regular tasks she manages in life and work, the calendar would be a cascading rainbow weekly. Many women's calendars are dominated by others' needs – family obligations, work demands, and caregiving responsibilities. This affirmation can help you see your calendar as a tool for your own prosperity rather than just a way to manage everyone else's priorities.

Consider these tips:

1. Create intentionality around time: Do you struggle to prioritize income-generating activities because they feel selfish, like taking time away from caring for others? This affirmation makes your prosperity planning a legitimate calendar priority and helps you to build systematic wealth habits. Prosperity requires consistent actions – tuning in, regular investing, networking, learning, skill development, and sometimes business activities. The calendar becomes the structure that ensures these prosperity-building activities actually happen rather than getting pushed aside.

2. Overcome the "I'll get to it later" pattern: Have you postponed your own financial goals indefinitely while handling the immediate demands of your family, work, or even friends? Do you feel caught by competing demands and even find yourself abandoning your own financial goals as a result? (Does this sound familiar: Sigh, "It will never happen.") This affirmation makes prosperity planning as important as any other scheduled commitment. Using the calendar as a prosperity tool creates order and ensures that wealth-building doesn't get lost in the chaos.

3. Make prosperity concrete: How clear are you on your own desire to build your wealth? (Step Five, again!) Abstract goals like "build wealth" can feel overwhelming and are not productive. When broken down into specific calendar actions, prosperity becomes achievable through daily and weekly commitments. Specific actions might look like this: 'Research on X-day what a Financial Advisor does.' 'Speak with trusted friends on X-day to ask about their financial advisors.' 'Look up and read about Mutual Funds on X-day.' 'Set up an appointment with my HR specialist to review my benefits on X-day. Make sure I'm making the best use of what is available for my long-term financial gain.' 'Schedule time to speak with life partner about our life insurance (or savings, or investments) on X-day.' 'Today, put $100 into IRA' ... can you see the pattern here? [NOTE: This book is not intended to be a deep-dive on financial mapping, just a motivator to tune in for prosperity consciousness.]

4. Create accountability: A scheduled commitment is more binding than a vague intention. This Affirmation helps you treat your prosperity activities with the same seriousness as other important appointments. Women are constantly in service to others, no? I get it, it's a natural (or learned?!) tendency. Making the calendar your friend to keep you on a prosperous track will help you to integrate the natural tendency to serve others with deliberate actions that build your own financial future. In this way, your calendar becomes a productive prosperity tool, rather than just a task manager.

5. Find a partner: This may be the single most important note in this entire book. Being alone can surely soothe the soul. But when it comes to productivity, having a trusted partner who cares about your success can make the ultimate difference. Showing up for each other, inspiring and motivating each other to keep on track and stay focused on your prosperity goals, using the calendar as your friend, will yield positive results in your accounts.

*Read my other 5 books to get your Self in sync, in balance, and in integral wellness! Look me up on Amazon to find all of my books: Susan Lowenthal Axelrod.

reflection

Do you get happy or stressed when you think about your calendar? Why? Imagine what could happen if you begin to think of the calendar as your friend, the greatest tool to build a road to meet your desired goals.

96 • Money flows freely to me.

CONCLUSION

Are you ready for financial flow?

Dear Friend,

We began this journey as strangers; now, after so much time spent and deep reflection, we are friends.

What a journey we have had here together! How have you done with all of this information and reflection?

Since I began this book project, I have been asking myself. 'What do I want people to do as a result of reading this book?' Now that we've been through it all, I know the answer clearly:

To have learned about Affirmations, how they work, and how they can support a prosperous mindset to generate financial flow.

To have a go-to library of Affirmations on this important topic. I have several books that I have had, used, and gone back to for years! I hope this will be one such book for you. Remember 'fail forward'? When that happens, come back to this book, to your reflections, and keep moving forward.

To commit to using any of the Affirmations that serve you. Committing is the thing.

To have more money in your financial accounts, to have investment accounts, to feel what wealth feels like. And,

To teach others what you have learned through the experience of this book.

Simple? I didn't say that. Possible? Yes, without a doubt, if you learn the prosperity consciousness secret:

What you focus on, you achieve. This is 100% guaranteed. <u>What you focus on, you achieve.</u> That is the reason I created this book/program.

To offer a guide to focus on your own finances, not avoid them, and to create financial flow. If you have gone through this book as a 12-Step Program, over dedicated days, weeks, or months, you will already be on the right track. Keep going.

Here's to your financial flow! Please stay in touch.

With love,

Susan

P.S. If you have found yourself struggling to stick with this program, or if you feel you would benefit from additional breakthrough work on old belief patterns, working with a Coach might be the answer. Feel free to contact me personally to discuss. 518-495-4573.

APPENDIX 1

Twelve Steps to Prosperity Consciousness

Step One: The Flow of Money

Money flows through my financial accounts.

Step Two: Conscious Abundance

I am open to receiving, there is enough.

Step Three: On Financial Flow

Financial abundance comes easily to me. I receive it with love, confidence, and gratitude.

Step Four: Surprise Yourself

I enjoy learning about finances and investments. I study one thing about money every day.

Step Five: Being Specific

My accounts are filled with the money I want.

Step Six: The Power of Thoughtful, Strategic, and Disciplined Action

I am thoughtful, strategic, and disciplined about activities that generate money flowing into my established accounts.

Step Seven: Be Accountable

I model financial responsibility for my children (for others).

Step Eight: Systems Yield Financial Progress

I set up a simple and effective system to support my prosperous growth and a resulting yield.

Step Nine: Practice, Practice, Practice

I learn about money every day.

Step Ten: Find Focus

Focus on what you want.

Step Eleven: Patience Pays Off

I take a long view for a prosperous return.

Step Twelve: Trust in Yourself

I believe I can.

BONUS Affirmation/Tool: Structure Leads to Success

The calendar keeps me on a prosperous track.

APPENDIX 2

For Group Conversation

Step One: The Flow of Money

Money flows through my financial accounts.

Reflection: What beliefs have I inherited about money being difficult, scarce, or "not for me?" How would my decisions change if I truly believed that money flows through my accounts with ease and purpose?

Step Two: Conscious Abundance

I am open to receiving, there is enough.

Reflection: In what area of your life do you most often feel there isn't enough or that it is hard to receive — money, time, energy, love, recognition? Consider this, then reflect, changing the idea from this: there isn't enough, to this: What would it feel like if there is enough? How would it feel to receive it easily?

Step Three: On Financial Flow

Financial abundance comes easily to me. I receive it with love, confidence, and gratitude.

Reflection: What would it feel like to be in an abundance mindset, to receive easily, and to know you will make good decisions about it from a place of informed personal confidence?

Step Four: Surprise Yourself

I enjoy learning about finances and investments. I study one thing about money every day.

Reflection: This Affirmation is not just about learning finance—it's about owning power, reclaiming personal space, and building legacy. For women, it turns financial literacy into an act of liberation and leadership. Can you feel it?!

Step Five: Being Specific

My accounts are filled with the money I want.

Reflection: Have I clearly defined how much money I want—and what I want it for? Or am I simply wishing for more?

Step Six: The Power of Thoughtful, Strategic, and Disciplined Action

I am thoughtful, strategic, and disciplined about activities that generate money flowing into my established accounts.

Reflection: In what specific area of your financial life have you been attributing your results to luck or external circumstances rather than recognizing your own strategic choices—and what would change if you fully owned that capability?

Step Seven: Be Accountable

I model financial responsibility for my children (for others).

Reflection: What comes up for you when you think of the term 'generational wealth'? Do you immediately say, "That's not me"? If so, that is what you are modeling for your children. What if you asked more neutrally, "Could I create generational wealth for my family going forward if I change the way I think about things and develop new practices and systems?" How does this resonate with you?

Step Eight: Systems Yield Financial Progress

I set up a simple and effective system to support my prosperous growth and a resulting yield.

Reflection: What systems can I put in place now to support my financial progress? And what internal beliefs or external habits might be preventing me from establishing them?

Step Nine: Practice, Practice, Practice

I learn about money every day.

Reflection: What practices am I ready to create for a prosperous, empowered mindset? How can I transform financial education into a daily lifestyle that builds long-term confidence and capability? Where is a good place to start my new practice of learning daily?

Step Ten: Find Focus

Focus on what you want.

Reflection: What do I truly want—not what I've been told to want, or what feels safe, or what others expect, but what I deeply and honestly desire? And how can I start focusing more clearly and consistently on that vision each day?

Step Eleven: Patience Pays Off

I take a long view for a prosperous return.

Reflection: How can I begin to trust the long view of my financial journey (remember Step 4)—and what can I do today that my future self will thank me for?

Step Twelve: Trust in Yourself

I believe I can.

Reflection: This affirmation is a quiet revolution. It's how you start to rewrite your financial story—not by waiting for the perfect time or conditions, but by deciding that your potential is real, right now. It's the mindset that turns hope into action—and action into prosperity. How do you want to start your next financial chapter? [Do you believe you can?]

BONUS Affirmation/Tool: Structure Leads to Success

The calendar keeps me on a prosperous track.

Reflection: Do you get happy or stressed when you think about your calendar? Why? Imagine what could happen if you begin to think of the calendar as your friend, the greatest tool to build a road to meet your desired goals.

APPENDIX 3
BONUS MEDITATION*

Your Journey to Prosperous Abundance

Open up to the world of abundance, of prosperity. Close your eyes, take a moment to stretch your shoulders and your neck, breathe gently, in and out, put your feet on the floor, and feel them firmly planted. Take another breath, deep breath in, long breath out.

It only takes a moment to break through the protective shield of scarcity that surrounds us. That feeling of 'there's never enough,' or 'I wish I had,' or 'if only.' It's comfortable; it's familiar, it's like a warm shroud that covers you, you hold it closely around your body.

**From Susan's book, Meditations to Ease, Calm, and Inspire: A Collection to Activate Your Mind and Soul, 2019.*

Except that shroud is suffocating you. Feel that now, there's a shortness of breath in the feeling of not enough.

Now, open up to the world of abundance, of prosperity; to the world of *there is enough*. Take a deep breath in and long breath out. And again, a deep breath in and long breath out

Feel yourself in this clear breathing space. Now, think of the light above your head that you imagine when you think of wealth, prosperity, abundance, and all things plentiful. When you think of these concepts, no doubt, you see them bathed in light.

Before we go on, I want to invite you to breathe good into that light that you see with your mind. Breathe the good from your heart, the good from your soul, into that light. Sometimes, that light can blind. Take a moment now to breathe, and breathe again.

Now that there is good in the light of prosperity and abundance, let's begin to imagine it can be ours. Bring that light in. Allow it to emanate and grow. Feel the light waves flow like ripples in the endless water. Imagine the light waves flowing outside of your body, outside of that small space in which you live, outside of the home, the block, the neighborhood, the greater community. Imagine the light waves rippling further, even than the community, to the state, across the country, rippling across the oceans throughout the world, beyond our world into the universe, and beyond the universe to become one with the greatest source. The greatest

Prosperous abundance is light in the form of love.

universal light source of energy that is. That light is prosperous abundance; it is currency in flow. Allow yourself to float there comfortably, peacefully, in total calm. Your body is floating, bobbing as if you are in the water, weightless, safe, surrounded by this universal, abundant light. It can be yours, it is yours.

What do you see? What do you feel? Are you floating among silver coins jingling underneath you? Are you lying on green bills softly cushioned around you? There is light in that prosperous abundance; it can be yours, it is yours. Imagine the money – fading out to light, and fading back in to money, and fading back out to light. It is one and the same. Prosperous abundance is light in the form of love. Invite this love in as self-love. You are worthy, no matter what, no matter what.

Breathe in the love; it can be yours, it is yours. This love and light and prosperous abundance can be yours;

it is yours. You can have it; it can be with you in every moment. Every moment that you think, 'There is enough.' 'I am enough.' This is self-energy.

Take a deep breath, breathe in the light and love and prosperity. 'There is enough.' 'I am enough.'

Let's return now. Back from the universe, back through the world, back across the oceans, back across the country, back through our community, our neighborhood, our street, our home, into the body.

You are back in your body, connected in love to the universal source, with self-energy. You are safe. Take a moment and think to yourself, 'I am safe.' 'I am love.' 'I am prosperous abundance.' 'It can be mine.' 'It is mine.' *This* is self-energy.

Breathe now and breathe again. Feel your body connected to the ground through your feet, tap your toes on the ground to feel grounded and centered. You are now centered and connected to prosperity; the currency, the light, and love that is enough. When you are ready, open your eyes. Welcome to your new world of prosperous abundance. It is yours. There is enough.

APPENDIX 4
BONUS AFFIRMATION

THE POWER OF PHILANTHROPY

I give generously to repair the world.

AAs you consider growing your own prosperous experience, there is one way that you can grease the spiritual wheels for improved outcomes. It's this: give money away.

"What?" you ask. "Give away money? I thought I was supposed to be saving and investing money!" Well, yes, that too, but there is a profound spiritual principle rooted in Jewish thought that when you give with generosity of spirit, it is returned to you manifold. The practice is called Tzedakah (tze-dahk-ah). Though literally translated as 'righteousness,' the generally accepted definition is 'act of charity.' This is my personal experience, and it is proven over millennia.

It is not just a Jewish concept, of course. In 1991, Methodist Minister Doug Lawson, PhD, wrote about it in his book, *Give to Live, How Giving Can Change Your Life*. I was just 6 years into my professional fundraising career, and I purchased the book and read it voraciously. In this book, Lawson offered "startling new information about the measurable, proven benefits you can gain from giving. These benefits include longer life, a lower level of stress, a stronger immune system, a stronger heart…greater emotional well-being, enhanced ability to cope with daily problems, and heightened appreciation of your own life." Personally, I can attest to every one of these positive outcomes from engaging with and supporting causes about which I feel passionate.

But one outcome that he did not write about, I have experienced myself. Giving generously to worthwhile causes with the intention of repairing the world, as if by magic, grows you prosperous returns. But it's not magic, it's your good spirit and output coming back to you in kind. I encourage you to test out this thesis personally. Dr Lawson is quite clear, and I agree, it is not about having or giving the most money, it is about giving what you can to repair the world with a pure heart.

As you consider the plight of others, do you feel somewhat powerless in the face of the daunting amount of need erupting everywhere that threatens the fabric of society? Engaging in giving generously is something you can do that fills you with positive power. If you are thinking to yourself, "But, I'm not wealthy, what

It is about giving what you can to repair the world with a pure heart.

difference can I make?" Understand this: Philanthropy is defined as "Goodwill to fellow members of the human race, especially active effort to promote human welfare; an act or gift done or made for humanitarian purposes." Philanthropy is something about which you have choice and total control – you choose where, when, and how you give. It is easy to do and the personal pay-off is great.

Your actions can make a difference, not just in the life of another person, but also for you.

When you Affirm, "I give generously to repair the world," and follow up the Affirmation with action, you will see prosperous returns over time. I have. I encourage you to try it and see for yourself.

WITH SUCH GRATITUDE

To Alina R. Haitz. Anyone in my line of work knows how lonely the work can be. Showing up, no matter what, never really knowing what's catching or what's not. For years, Alina has shown up in support of my work, and I'm grateful. After I had started this book, I stalled. I realized that it would be helpful to have someone to work with for support and accountability. Through social media, I invited anyone to apply, and Alina responded! I was delighted because I knew her well, how smart she was, and the quality of her work. Working together, she helped me get through a big hump, reviewing material and sourcing AI as appropriate. Without her, I don't think this book would have come to fruition.

To my sister, Laura Lowenthal Bly. For more years than I can count, Laur has been sharing materials with me that came across her screen. Early on, in my consciousness journey, I made a decision that I could learn from my younger sister. Why not? What does birth order have to do with soul seeking and soul rising? One such share was a program released in 1994 by Nightingale Conant. It was a recorded cassette tape series from a LIVE course taught by Fredric Lehrman, called Prosperity Consciousness, How to Tap Your Unlimited Wealth. This was at least 25 years ago, and I have since been on the path to an enlightened frame of mind around money, abundance, and prosperity. With gratitude to my sister for decades of dedicated support for my life and business endeavors, XXOOS.

To the Jewish Girls Unite Women's Leadership Group of 2017, under the leadership and vision of Nechama Dina Wasserman Laber. Thank you for your attention to this material; thank you for your trust. Baruch Hashem for your perseverance, dedication, and passion for bringing Heaven down to Earth, and helping our Jewish daughters become Jewish mothers.

To my other sibs, Anne and Mike. I'm entirely grateful for your deep and abiding support through my journey of change, allowing me to be who I am becoming. I am witness to change in each of you, and it is honestly breathtaking (the grandchildren are watching us). Mom and Dad's legacy is secure in the four of us. Also, with appreciation, the legacy of MMA, ESSA, RSL, and ML.

To Fredric Lehrman. I'm grateful for the time, effort, and energy you put into creating this seminal work that changed my life. I have paid that energy forward many times over, and will continue to do so as long as I live. I hope others will also take up the gauntlet and pass it forward to future generations. Prosperity Consciousness, How to tap your unlimited wealth, 1994.

To my daughters. If there were just one Affirmation in this entire book that I could be sure you would integrate, it would be Step 12, the final step, I believe I can. Believe it, you Can. ILYXXOOM

ABOUT THE AUTHOR

Confident-Life™
Imagine the Possibilities.

Susan Axelrod, CCP, TIPC is the go-to Confidence Coach for Women and for Young Professionals. Specializing in working with executive women and matriarchs in mid-life who have spent decades doing for others and are now starting businesses or other personal endeavors in their 'second half.' And now, working in earnest with Young Professionals with straight talk, in a safe and sacred space for a more sure and secure future.

Using co-creative & co-facilitative coaching methods, Susan helps clients uncover the inspired Soul within who is looking to live out life in a self-fulfilling and purposeful way. Susan doesn't give answers or advice. She works with clients to delve into their core, exploring the girl she was, and the woman she wants to be for the rest of her life, personally, professionally, spiritually, and physically. Using original Confident-Life™ Tools, Susan helps women find the Clarity and Confidence they seek. She works with women who declare themselves 'READY!' ...ready to GROW, to live now, in spiritual self-connection, and to create a meaningful legacy. Susan's contagious enthusiasm and deep listening skills spark and motivate clients to get Confident and thrive.

Looking for Motivational Speaking or Workshops? Susan's Confident-Life Workshops™ and speaking engagements are a hit every time! Available for work-teams, book clubs, friend groups, women CEO clubs, nonprofits, or any place women gather. Using Tai Chi and Qigong as a basis to connect to Self, Susan weaves mindfulness and conscious awareness into everything she does.

Certifications:

- Certified Coach Practitioner, through The Coach Training Academy [accredited by the International Coaching Federation and Certified Coaches Alliance].
- Trauma-Informed Professional Coach, certified through Lodestar.
- Qigong & Tai Chi Easy Level 1 & Level 2 Teacher, certified by the Institute of Integral Qigong & Tai Chi. Certificate in Medical Qigong, issued by the Institute of Integral Qigong & Tai Chi.

Other Books - Available on Amazon:

100% of the proceeds from these books support the global organization co-founded by the author, Jewish Girls Unite jewishgirlsunite.com

ARE YOU READY TO LIVE A MORE CONFIDENT-LIFE™?

Contact Susan now, you'll be glad you did. When you call, Susan responds. Everything is timely, 100% personal and 100% custom. Connect personally now for coaching, or to bring a Confident-Life Workshop™ or Motivational Speaker to your group. Learn about Susan and her work here: www.whatwillyourlegacybe.com.

CONTACT: susan@confident-life.com | 518-495-4573

I truly love to connect personally with my readers, I look forward to 'seeing you' anywhere!

- Look me up on FB or LinkedIn by my name, Susan Axelrod!
- Here's my FB biz page: 'What Will Your Legacy Be?'
- Here's my FB group: 'Discovering You Again for women in the second half of life'
- Here's my website: www.whatwillyourlegacybe.com
- My body of work lives on my YouTube Channel: The Confidence Zone with Coach Susan Axelrod. Type this into any search engine: youtube susan axelrod @ confidence zone
- Find my 5 books on Amazon, Author name-Susan Lowenthal Axelrod

www.ingramcontent.com/pod-product-compliance
Lightning Source LLC
LaVergne TN
LVHW022108200926
848481LV00003B/1100
9798218853167